The Space
Between the Syllables

★ ———————————————————— ★

PAUL BURA

Evergreen Books
EDINBURGH

◯ Paul Bura, 1979

Made and printed in Great Britain
by Caithness Books, Thurso
from composition by
Alacrity Phototypesetters,
Banwell Castle, Bristol
and published by
EVERGREEN BOOKS
2, 3 & 4 Abbeymount
Edinburgh 8

OTHER BOOKS BY PAUL BURA

Just Another Poet
Mustn't Dent the Memory
Behind the Joker
From Under the Stairs (*Bosgo Publications*)
The Coming of the Giants (*Mitre Press*)

Contents

FIVE WAS A GOOD YEAR

It seems so ridiculous
That I could have been that young,
That I had no worry of getting old.

I wasn't going to school,
I was going to be a fisherman.
At least that's what I told my mother.
She had other ideas.

When I went out lobster fishing with Pop*
I caught a big fish.
Looking back I like to remember
That it was I that caught that fish
And Pop hadn't put it on my line.

When we pulled in at Neptune Jetty
I jumped ashore and grabbed the rope,
Tied up quickly before some other kid beat me to it.
That was important.
How else could I prove to Pop
That I was a great fisherman... and a man?

I had a green cloak braided with gold
And with it I would fly
                    down
                        from
                            the
                                trees
And fight off the boys
Who were after those precious birds' eggs.
I practised jumping off my bed wearing my green cloak.

* Pop Prestly was an old fisherman that I knew. To me he was
God. He was also known as "Ninety" because even as a young
man he always appeared to be "moaning like an old man of
ninety".

I never learnt how to fly
But I believed I could.

I fell in love when I was five
And I think she loved me too.
I used to give her presents:
Half a pencil, an old coin
And a book so she could draw rings.
Sometimes I gave her a sweet.
I never gave my sweets to anyone else.
I loved her ... honest.

When I was seven I grew up
For it was then I realised
How good it was
To be five.

BETWEEN FIVE AND SEVEN

I was six,
So was she.

She filled my school-long life,
I would have died for her.

I scaled mighty cliffs,
Six foot high, to win her.
I cleared chasms with
A single bound!

(I hurt my back but I
never told her, I could
not admit to pain!)

I was superman,
I was HER man.

I and my friends
Hauled a great log
From the sea, tied ropes
To it, dragging it, like
Egyptian slaves, under the
Burning Herne Bay sun.

She was there, watching.
Never before or since
Did I feel more like a man,
More like a love-slave.

She stayed only one more term,
Then left.

My heart went with her,
My manhood too.

THE THREEPENNY PIECE
AND OTHER RELATED BITS

It burned my hand
That threepenny bit:
I placed it carefully
On the old brick wall
In Brunswick Street.

My Father's voice:
"Never take money from strangers!"
Something awful would happen
If I disobeyed; what I didn't know.

But the man had insisted
And anyway I did know the man
As a friend of my Father.

That threepenny bit
Would have bought a whole
Tub of Macari's ice cream.

Guilt and fear tore at me.

So I placed it carefully
On the old brick wall
In Brunswick Street
And walked away.

Who would find it
And wonder why?

Where is that threepenny bit now?
Called back by time to the melting-pot?
Like a soul back to God.

*　　　*　　　*

Uncle Max
Bought me a fishing rod
That lay on my Iron Lung
Whilst destiny still wrestled
With the Polio thing.

That rod was a symbol
Of all that I had left behind,
All that I would return to.

I never told you, Uncle Max,
But here, twenty-seven years later:
                    Thank you.

                *   *   *

My parents showered my bed
With presents and gifts:
Steak and chips in a vacuum,
Aeroplanes that flew,
Books that I never read.

Most of the kids got nothing
Not even parents.

I was embarrassed;
I was only eight
But I was so embarrassed.

"Please don't bring me
Any more presents."

They didn't.
I felt better.

                *   *   *

I fell in love
With Nurse Roberts and Nurse Henderson.
I didn't know about sex, but I was getting close!

MICKEY SPEARIE'S POEM

Mickey Spearie ruled
Our hospital ward like a King.
As a new recruit we had to be vetted
By Mickey; given the okay.

We were all under his wing,
Like a brood of limping, helpless chicks.

Even the nurses respected him.

Mickey was twelve; the eldest.
We were a strange, crippled crew of kids:

Little Pam
Strapped in her wheelchair.
A rubber bottle swung beneath her
Like a deflated udder
To catch the waste she couldn't feel.

Rosemary, only six,
Woken every morning at seven without fail.
They had to exercise her limbs or she couldn't move.
Rheumatism at six years old;
An old lady who would never know
What it was to be young.

Me, wheelchair-bound but hopeful:
Already a caliper and a plastic spinal-jacket,
Already clinging upright to bedrails.

Mickey just sat and watched,
Encouraging us all. Called us cowards
When three steps seemed like a mile.

"When are YOU going to walk, Mickey?"
"One day," he said, "one day."

Mickey's body was curled round like a spring.
Sometimes he would demonstrate
How tall he was by trying to
Stretch his body the full length of the bed.
Everybody admired how tall he was.

All he knew of the world
Was a big cushion
That was his home,
Placed in front of the window
That overlooked a harbour.
"Perhaps I'll skipper a boat, one day!"

It was visiting day;
All the parents were there.
My big day had arrived; I was going home!
I did the rounds saying goodbye,
Clutching my new sticks.
Mickey's mother just sat
And looked at me, her eyes full.

Mickey said HE would be going home one day.

He lived to be seventeen.
Mickey never walked.

I learned from him
That you don't need
To know how to walk
In order to be a leader.
All you need is the ability
To draw strength from weakness.

Mickey had that ability,
And gave it till he died.

FIRST STEP

Wearing a caliper
And spinal-brace was one thing,
Walking was another.

The "Big Man" was coming:
Today I had to demonstrate
That I could walk unaided,
Prove that home was just a footstep away.

Each in turn
Paraded in front of the "doctor",
Each in turn giving their version
Of walking, walking without holding on!

My turn.

I was terrified.
A nurse held me, pointed me.
I clutched her like a drowning man.

The doctor waited,
Six feet of infinity lay between us.
I felt as though I had to leap
Off a high cliff
Hoping desperately that I would fly.

I hesitated; the silence deafened me.

Suddenly I felt as though someone
Had pushed me, as if an inner me,
More powerful than I, had taken over:
I was walking... by myself.

Perhaps "staggering" was a better word.

I fell into the arms of the doctor.
"There," he said, "I knew you could do it."

Maybe I was more scared
Of losing face in front of my mates,
I don't know. Whatever it was, it worked...
        and I'm still doing it!

THROUGH MY SISTER MELLY

Big eyes
And dirty knees,
Hair long and wild,
Her height level with my shoulder.

I was twelve, she was nine.
Every day she'd push me
Up Beltinge Hill on my
Huge tricycle, my little
Brother tagging along,
Dragging his five years behind.

A good long push
Would send me sailing uphill
For a few yards or so
Whilst I harnessed what strength
I had in pushing the pedals round.

She never complained.

After the day's school
Was at an end came our reward:

I pushed the tricycle out
And pointed it down the hill.
One small push and two kids
Crammed themselves on to the back axle
Making a total of three screaming maniacs
Hurtling down Beltinge Hill!
At the traffic lights we stopped,
My tousle-haired little sister
Ran back to stamp up and down
On the rubber strip to make the lights change.

My elder sister said
That we whispered secrets together,
My younger sister and I.
She admitted to being a little jealous
And maybe she had every right to be.

Little sister Melly
Was my test pilot; she
Would do all the things

That I couldn't and I would
See and experience all these things
Through her.
A word from me would send her
And my brother scuttling down
The cliffs, a rope tied round a tree
And fastened to my wheelchair.
Sledges and box-carts I constructed,
Machines that I could never ride.
But I did — through my sister Melly.

The years lay stretched and worn now,
Our childhood and destiny ever wider.

A month or so ago
I purchased another large tricycle.
Maybe, in some way, I wanted to go back.
Riding it now was hard work.

Roping it to the roof of my car
I took it to Worthing...
Where my dirty-kneed little sister
Resprayed it.

Now it is *she* who does the riding
And, as a poet,
It is I who do the dreaming.

LOOKING FOR WALKING STICKS

I stopped the car
At the edge of the wood
And walked with invalid care
Through the twisted beauty
That rang the changes
Yet never changed.

I collected fallen sticks,
Twisted by natural design,
That I could preserve for
A hundred years, sticks that
Would take the weight off a man
Just by looking at them.

It was there, always there,
And I touched it again!

The trees shouted at me;
The wood rang with words.

When I can see the universe
Through one eye, feel it move
In the palm of my hand;
When I no longer answer
To a name — because I have no name —
Then I will have come home.

DAY IN THE LIFE OF

A Kamika(r)ze-bird
Expired at 20 miles an hour
On the flank of my car.

The traffic in London
Like a force-field
Against time and appointments.

Arrived late at the studio.
(A previous place of disaster for me.)
The cold in my legs
Gave way to dull pain
As the floor came up to meet me.
Strong arms muffled my apologies.
I recorded the story; the studio were pleased:
Unasked-for praise rang
In my ears   .
And promises were already gathering dust.

Back along the Edgware Road
I saw Jay,
I swear I saw Jay:
Standing on a corner
(Wearing glasses now) —
I thought he was in Australia!
Hadn't seen him for fifteen years!

Victoria Station.
Jennie held the little deaf girl
By the hand — the last of the school
Party to be collected.
Lunch in Victoria Station.

Two men
And a beautiful Dutch girl
Hunched in a circle
Plotting a revolution?
The flamboyant Irishman

Poured Guinness,
Listening to the lady
From Glasgow.

The little deaf mute collected
(After warming herself in my coat).

We visited the Tate,
Befriended an attendant
(Not forgetting Constable)
Who provided a guided wheelchair
Complete with warm wit.

Oh, you paintings!
Why has it taken me so long
To know of you?

How blind and mute
I have been these years,
And will that little girl
Know anything of what I have seen
This one day in my life?

DANGEROUS SMILE

He came towards me,
Nodding and gesturing,
Smiling at everyone
That he met.

In the distance
I could just make out
A badge pinned to his lapel.
He continued to smile and nod
His way towards me.

Soon it would be my turn.

I was afraid:
He must be mad.
He might try to speak with me.
Should I cross the road,
Avoiding his smile, his gaze?

Too late —
He was upon me
And the badge spoke instead.
            It read:
"SMILE AT SOMEONE
THE WORLD HAS NEED OF IT."

I failed the test.

FOR THE MAN WHO KICKS PIGS
(For Bernard)

There were a line of them
All penned in, all eyes.
Beautiful to look at
And very easy to kill.

Death lay around like gas,
And they could smell it.
Fear was in their eyes; tears too.

Did you know a cow can cry?
Oh yes, quite easily,
Just like you and I,
Before a firing squad, ready to die!

Did you ever hear
Of a plant that grows flesh?
They call it a pig:

>   Never knowing the pleasure of sex,
>   Only a tube that gives life,
>   The young never knowing
>   What it is to feel the warmth of their mother,
>   her love.

>   Born to grow in a box.
>   Never feeling the earth.
>   Never knowing sunlight.
>   Fed on liquids, their weight monitered.

>   Suddenly it's time!
>   Hardly knowing what it is to walk,
>   The box opens, sticks prod and push,
>   Daylight bursts into unused eyes (pain already).

The misery of not knowing, not understanding.
Suddenly herded in with their own kind,
Touching, smelling, moving fast somehow.
Sticks prodding and pushing again:

Down the ramp. Distant screams.
The strange, musty smell of fear.
Sudden death... but no life.

I worked with an ex-slaughterman.
I didn't hate him; I loved the old man.
It·was just a job to him;
He never really thought about it.

That's just it:
Nobody thinks about it.
It might go away.

It doesn't.

Cows, pigs and sheep
Look nice in fields, don't they?
At least here they know life.

When we die
They put us in a box;
When a pig is *born*
They put *it* in a box.

A WASTED LIFE
(True account: for Roger)

The interviewer,
Microphone in hand,
Tape ready to reel,
Sat down at the table
Where the old man sipped tea.

Interviewer:	Tell me about yourself.
Old Man:	Nothing to tell.
Interviewer:	Where do you live?
Old Man:	In a home.
Interviewer:	Old folks' home?
Old Man:	Naw, mental home. Been there all me life; got to go now.
Interviewer:	Why? Got to be back on time?
Old Man:	Naw; do what I like. Must go now.
Interviewer:	Why, if you can do what you like?
Old Man:	It's my friend, it's Billy; must take him to tea.
Interviewer:	Why?
Old Man:	He's blind. We're friends. I always take 'im to tea.

The interviewer,
Microphone in hand,
Switched off his machine.
Later, in a moment of guilt,
He erased the tape.

RETIREMENT

Jack retired today:
The lads had a whip-round
And the firm gave him a clock
To tick away what remained
Of his life; elegantly inscribed, mind,
Even if they did spell his name wrong.
The managing director made a speech.
He didn't get the name wrong, he
Forgot it altogether: a whisper
In a reddened ear, the clearing
Of a nervous throat. What did it matter?

A toast.
A round of applause.
Slaps on the back.
"Lucky old Jack."

Fifty years: man and boy.
Fifty years: a wife, two sons.
Fifty years: a council house.
Fifty years: a steel worker.
Fifty years: walked three miles there, three miles back.
Fifty years: off work only once, with 'flu.

The last walk home.
Jack could do it blindfold.
Fifty years of shoe-leather
Lay in the dust along the lane;
Fifty bloody years!

There in front of him, a sign:
            "KEEP CLEAR. TREE UNSAFE!"
A group of men with
Ropes and axes
Stood underneath a huge elm tree:
"I never noticed
That tree before," thought Jack.

Come to think of it
He didn't recognise anything!

Oh, it was the same lane,
The road to and from work,
But somehow different.
The elm tree was so big, so beautiful —
Why hadn't he seen it before?
Those wild flowers near the hedge ... beautiful.

The ropes stretched,
The winch gathered strength.
The elm tree groaned!

Jack stood stock still, eyes wide,
His gifted clock clutched to his side:
He had no ears or eyes for time now.

The elm tree groaned.

"Keep clear, old man!"
"Old man?" thought Jack.
"Am I old now? Does it show?"

Jack looked up at the tree,
His mind screaming:
"I never got to know you, Tree;
It has taken my whole life to see you!"
The tree lurched and groaned.

Jack showed the clock to his wife.
He never told her about the tree, mind;
She would never have understood.

Had he really understood?
How could a tree talk?
But he had heard it, quite distinctly,
Almost like a violin, it said:
        "But I have seen you, Jack,
            We retire today, you and I!"

First broadcast on BBC Radio.

A FEW WORDS FOR HUGH
(For Hugh Wightman)

When you die
In the twinkling of an eye
You see it all again,
Every facet of your life:
The ups and downs,
The success and failures,
The loves and hates.
All, all of it.
Quite natural; lets you know
How you stand in the order of things.

I was a part-time car park attendant.
One day a week in the company
Of a man I grew to love.

Hugh was a sixty-Players-a-day man
(eighty if the truth were known);
At the end of the day,
After eight hours with Hugh in the hut,
I smelt like an unwashed ashtray!
I didn't care. (Always gave me a cheese roll
And a cup of tea, morning and afternoon.)

As the years rolled by I learnt
That he had been a slaughterman,
A chef; had his own small haulage firm;
Rented out radio sets for extra money;
A fireman in London during the war;
And finally forty years as a bus driver
For London Transport where he perfected
The art of concealing a cigarette
Whilst driving through London, a brown
Stain like a stigmata on the palm of his hand.

Never allowed himself to see the inside
Of a Labour Exchange. Not his style.

It's easy to say
That he was a kind man (he was),

Easy to say that he will
Be missed, easy to say
All the things that people
Say when you've gone.

If I were to say that he
Barked at a few folk and
Upset them without knowing;
If I were to say that he'd give
You the shirt off his back
If you were down... but never talk
To you again if you betrayed him...
You would say: "So what; so what?
So-and-so was like that."

Well okay.

He was seventy-four; I was thirty-two.
We were the best god-damned team
Ever to grace a car park.
Every Christmas we'd receive bottles
Of wine, cigars and cash, cards —
Just because we were civil to folk:
Gave them a smile and wished them good-day.
We bounced off one another.

(He went quietly sad over Christmas
  when I whistled *Away in a Manger,*
  he told me not to whistle it 'cos
  it reminded him of his little daughter
  who had died some years before.)

I'm not going to give you
All that "Great-car-park-in-the-sky" stuff.
I like to remember him singing
One of his naughty songs, or a quiet
Irish folk song — oh yes, he was
An Irishman — or just taking the
Mickey by singing:
        ("Ol' Paul Bura
          Is an old *" &+!")

27

He made me laugh,
That's a quality
That reigns large in my life.

> "I derived my ability
> From my grandfather Dan:
> I'm geometrical, geographical,
> I'm a knowledgeable man...
> Stuff that in yer bloody pipe and smoke it!"

I don't know what it means
But he said it all the time.

When he went into hospital
After his first stroke
He told his wife:

> "Tell Paul where I am."

Maybe I will remember him most
For remembering me.

NEVER TOO LATE TO LEARN

His eyes were bright and quizzical
Amongst the twisted tangle
Of plastic tubing sustaining life.

He was quite mute,
Seeming not to hear, feel or understand.

And all the while, all the while
The old elm tree tapped at the window
And sighed its way inside him:
His eyes sped to the window,
The head and body remaining still.

He saw not a tree
But a bright glowing thing
That touched a part of him
That in walking days
He never knew.

Everything around him was a shadow.

But the tree "knew" him
And he acknowledged that "knowing",
Yet a nurse's cool hand he never felt.

When morning came with all its promises
The tree tapped as usual,
Greeting him in the light of day.
And as he looked he saw
The tree's light grow dim
And pain filled his body like poison.

The old woodsman screamed,
He screamed amidst his mess of tubes,
Screamed for the loss of his friend,

Screamed for the reality that now
Crowded and clawed its way back.

He looked toward the window
But the tree had gone.

The old elm had a disease too.

First published by Fauxpas Publications.

WHAT CAN YOU DO FOR ME, YOUNG MAN?

(An alcoholic I knew, dying of cancer)

So what
Can you do for me, young man,
What can you do for me?
I who have a cancer,
Crisp as bells,
Its rifle-eye pointing
Only six months away!

Why do I drink?
What made me an alcoholic?

I killed four men!
Oh, don't look so surprised;
I did it within the law.
I was a Prison Officer.

Remember young Craig?
It was *I* who led him up the scaffold,
I who watched him drop
Only one breath away!
Every day for weeks
He asked me, this young lad,
"Is it today, mister; is it today?"

I helped top five in all,
Including a girl,
Yet I only remember one name.
How strange it all is.

Maybe they
Deserved to die,
Maybe they had
It coming.

But did *I* deserve
To kill *them*?

Stopping my ears up
Or unstopping a bottle

Doesn't shut out his voice:
"Is it today, mister; is it today?"
So what
Can you do for me, young man,
What can you do for me?

First published by Excello & Bollard.

THE WISH GRANTER

All day
They came and went,
Their one, single wish fulfilled:

The lame walked,
The blind saw,
The poor received riches,
The homeless property,
The hungry food,
The drunkard wine.
Many a wish led only to misery
But nothing was too much.

The sun set.
The Wish Granter stood alone now;
His eyes were sad and tired.

A young man approached.

"What is your wish?" asked the Wish Granter.
The young man replied:
"My desire is to be a Wish Granter like you
That I may have the gift of giving."

The Wish Granter paused,
Then, taking off his shoes
He handed them to the young man.
"These shoes were made for us both.
My work is done; yours is about to begin."

Where the Wish Granter had stood
Was nothing but the imprint of his bare feet!

THE WAY TO SAY GOOD-BYE
(My Great-grandmother's dog)

The hole took shape
Day by day.
Nobody took much notice.
Why should they?
Dogs do it all the time.

Three days passed.
The hole was completed.

He padded from room to room
Pausing just long enough...
Just long enough.

A gentle nose
Nuzzled each and every one of us.
A single, longing glance
Was all it took.

Then out into the garden,
Filling the hole with his warmth,
Welcoming the earth
As an old friend.

No fuss.

Here then was
The way to say good-bye.

THROUGH THE INTELLECT

I need a little agony again
Or the poignancy of my words
Becomes unreal.

For all those who wallow
Only in the intellect
And find the words
        Love, tears and *passion*
Nauseating —
You do not truly feel.
Let pain and love touch you,
Be it only briefly,
And see how much you learn.
Then perhaps you will write
A love poem for the first time,
Take a stranger in your arms,
Cry without shame because
The world moves you.

Through the intellect
You will store enough knowledge
To build a galaxy,
But the path to the Infinite
Will always evade you.

I GLIMPSED ETERNITY
AND SAW A FRIEND THROUGH NEW EYES

We are not brothers
You and I, my friend.
The distance between
Our blood and nature
Is measured in light years,
Yet our spirit is bonded
By something beyond reason.

In seeing you now
In this time and place,
I have glimpsed Eternity,
For you will never wither and fade;
Never die.

Oh, I may lose sight of you,
Maybe worlds will split us for a while,
But as the streams find the river,
Again and again,
So then shall we meet
Until the Father of all things deems it right
That we may draw breath again,
Turn over an old memory or two
Of a time past: the women we have loved
And how long it takes to know what love is.

Though we may weep a hundred years
Yet will it be
But a drop of rain on the window-pane.

I FEEL EMOTION

I feel emotion
Much more acutely now.
The older I get
The easier it becomes.
I well up at
The simplest of things:
      other people's happiness,
      children explaining things,
      a reassuring hand on a shoulder,
      a smile carefully placed,
      the words *hello, thank-you* and *good-bye*,
But more, much more.

I cannot help it
And I do not excuse it.
Yet I feel I must
Exercise more control
To save others embarrassment.

It is a luxury none the less,
And people who deny it,
Who claim they have no need of it,
Simply deceive themselves.

It is a "sweet pain"
But, used as a weapon,
More devastating than an earthquake.

KNOCK ME DOWN

You can knock
Me down with a thought
And you'll never know it.
I'll harbour it for days,
Wrestling with the right or wrong of it,
Aware that a string has been plucked —
An old string vibrating fear,
Uncovering a whole symphony
Of self-doubt.

But it clears me out
Like a mental laxative;
Sets a firmer foundation
For all the things
That I hold dear.

When I come back to you
I will be a stronger man
Though still on my guard
Against any foe-thought
That breaks up my day.

In the end, perhaps,
I will have to admit:
You were right!

THE SPACE BETWEEN THE SYLLABLES

There is no value
In looking back.
If the lesson has taken hold
Then it becomes part
Of today; today is
The spring-board for tomorrow.
Having left the spring-board
You can look back and still
See it vibrating...
But the leap you have already made.

I have sat in this blackness
Now for three months: laughter
Now is hard to imitate.

Although the blackness
Was a despair so deep that
I could see no end,
I still felt, again, that
Here was something else
To swim through... or drown.

I regret none of it.
The tears I wept uncontrollably
On the shoulders of my mother
And sister were real enough.
The feelings that motivated them
I have yet truly to understand.
There is more fear in me than
I know; more things that make
Me a heaven and earth...

Poetry does not
Always have to carve the answer;
It should also ask questions.
I am a poet and question myself always;
Therefore questions should be
As important as the answers.

(What is it that you seek, poet?)
(I seek the space between the syllables.)
(What is that space?)
(Today I know the answer, tomorrow I shall
    forget.)
(How so?)
(It is not Truth that changes but our under-
    standing of it.)

I could not have known
That I would write any of this:
My typewriter obeys me
And I obey something else.
I do not question it
Any more than I question
The space between the syllables.

AFTER READING A POEM
BY HERMANN HESSE

So then,
What am I?
A poet who can
Only echo words
That have been uttered
A million times.

If I am able
To find some chord,
Some area or dimension
Yet unexplored,
Then I shall cease to write,
For I presume too much!
Better that I lay
My pen down in finality;
Better that I cease now!

But what then?

Every poet knows
What I know;
Every man who possesses
An ounce of creativity
Knows this pain,
But knowing it
He continues to strive.
He has to,
Even if only to catch up!

PREPARATION

It has to be a preparation,
All these years.
I have to believe that
Or lay my pen and self down
In finality.

But what I do not know.

The higher part of me
Drives me on to an
Invisible but supreme "destiny-point"
That my whole life
Was designed for.

It comes sometimes
As a strange breeze,
Something I can almost smell,
A forgotten taste,
A familiar road
That I cannot tread.

I have it all here, right here,
Yet I cannot tell you what it is,
Nor dare even try.

I do not believe
That when at last
My beard turns pure white
And the virgin page stays virgin,
I will look back and say:
  "Christ! What a mess!"

SEEDS

Earth had gathered in a corner
Of the time-worn stone;
Here a daisy seed was sown
By the hands of a destiny-wind.
Did the seed have a choice?

Was the wind ordained
To find a womb for it to grow,
Or did a greater Wind blow
Far beyond the minds of men?

How many of us
Choose earth's little acre
To nestle and grow?
How great was the wind
That blew me here
To plant my words
In the soil of minds
I may never know?

BOOK OF POEMS

I stumbled across it:
A thin, worn collection of poems
Privately published with blooded
Sweat and proud anticipation.

Hawked around bookshops;
Posted to all the magazines.
Finally, given away
To anyone who showed interest.

I could feel the sorrow,
The torment, the anguish
Of this poet whose only wish
Was to ignite some soul with words.

To this day his poems elude
My understanding, yet his rhythms haunt me;
The vibration of his words
Draws me to his side.

From the man who printed his work
I learned that leukaemic blood finally
Pushed his spirit from its tomb.
I hold in my hands his epitaph.

HOW MANY BOOKS?

It's autumn now
And '76 has been a bad year.
Yet on reflection
Perhaps not so bad.
I tend to measure time
In gigs* and money
And how many books
I sold this year.
It shouldn't be like that.

This year
I should see
As the Year of the Ladies:
I have felt such warmth and love
That I could write a book,
Though a poem will do.

I think I became a poet
Because I'm a lazy writer:
I like to get things done quickly,
Without fuss, and if I can create
An army, a hero or two, show light,
Love and salvation in a few lines,
String out a few emotions that
You pretend you don't have,
Then what I'm doing is right
And I'm glad to be lazy.

This summer came soon and easy
And I soaked up more sun
In a week than I have in years.
Maybe I thought the heat would
Melt and remould my body straight again
So again I could be

* One-night poetry readings.

Five years old,
Running along the shore,
Wetting my feet,
Letting the sea love me again,
Lifting rocks and fishing
With mussels and a piece of string.
No envy at work here, only memory;
My body serves me now in different ways.
I love more at a distance now, that's all.

How beautiful women are:
1976 has shown me
That there is no type or size
That does not please me, no
Length of hair — corn or ebony —
That can stop me from
Reaching out and touching.
Jeans covered in sheep-shit,
Tight on the hip; chiffon
Over naked breasts,
All is beauty.

How many books
Sold in '76?
How many perfumes
Still hide in my smock?
'76 has been a good year
And I'll not forget.

LETTERS

So you nearly wrote
To me?

Why didn't you?

If my poems
Got through to you
Then telepathy is not enough.

I need to know.
Not for reasons of ego
(I keep telling myself)
But just pure communication.

We all share the same things,
When it comes down to it,
And I'm not different from you.

Drop me a line
And see what happens.

(This poem is a poet's way
      of saying:

            "If you're pretty and lonely
            and preferably female,
            how about dinner?")

SOMETIMES I WANT

Sometimes I want
Just to soar into you,
To feel every part of you
All at one time:
The weight of your breasts,
The down of your belly,
The eagerness of your mouth.
A kind of physical "oneness".

My lovemaking
Is a sort of compromise:
It's all there in my head
But this body was not built
To respond to all the brain
Impulses; therefore *you* become
My compromise, taking up the
Positions that should be mine.

I'll never carry you over any threshold,
Nor lay you covered in sunshine and flowers
On a lovers' bed;
Instead it will have to be a poem
And a poem and yet another poem.
You will wear them like
A lover's scar
And see them fade
In the light of a shadow
That is forever mine.

WHAT MOVES YOU?

What moves you?
If the world
Had a price tag
I would pay it
Just to show you the real things.

Rocks are more than
Just rocks, you know,
And the rain has a caress
If you look hard.

I have yet to write
A poem that means
More to you than words on paper,
Yet you stay with me. Why?

What moves you?

That final moment in bed?
The long sigh?
The hot tea after
With the rain and wind
Beating from the outside?
All these things are real to me,
Yet you just smile
And give me your hand,
Lay your head in my lap
And sleep.

Maybe it is I
That do not understand.
Some things cannot
Be written down or talked about.
Perhaps all along
I just needed reassuring
That you loved me
When I should have known
From your eyes

And the way you touch me
That you do.

I have much to learn from you.
We are not all poets
And yet you are a greater poet
Than I will ever be.

What moves you?

Perhaps all along
You were content
In just knowing
That we moved each other.

What more is there to say?

SHE LOVED ME ONCE

She loved me once, this lady,
    When my poems were tall and grand;
Now she just nods in agreement
    Or dismisses with a wave of her hand.

You loved me then, remember?
    You loved *me*, ol' poetic Paul?
But now my words mean nothing,
    Absolutely nothing to you at all.

I wouldn't mind if you hated what I could not give,
    I wouldn't mind, wouldn't mind one scrap,
But to say that my poems now mean nothing
    Says that all along... they were crap!

First published by Excello & Bollard.

THE ULTIMATE IN SHARING

Some of my best poems
Sail into me through emotions.

Somehow sadness has
A strange beauty
As though there is
A need in me to express
Myself with tears, to
Demonstrate that I have
Not forgotten how to feel.

With certain ladies
Hard embraces, soft caresses
Are not enough.
I need to consume, to devour,
Take that person into myself;
Make them a part of me.
It is, perhaps, a spiritual thing,
Making the body clumsy,
An impassable bridge; but if
The feeling is deep enough, and mutual,
Then the bridge will disappear
And the chasm that it spanned
Will not exist, the two sides
Fusing, coming together.

Surely this is the ultimate in sharing?

FOR THE BUTTERFLY LADY
(For S.)

I know you so well
Yet I know you not at all.

I have watched your dark eyes
Shine when Truth is near
And I have seen them laugh
When humour — so much a part of you —
Bubbles over.

I listen to your stories
And see how earnest you are
As they flow here and there
For anyone to touch,
And gifts you leave like Santa Claus.

You lay in my arms
And I matched you breath for breath,
Felt your body jerk in small spasms
As sleep took you from me
And released you to me again in the dawn.
I travelled your body without a map
Using your touch as my compass.

I see you for a night
Just once a year
And still you manage to fill a part of me.

The coloured streamers that you
Hung about our bed
And those that I found inside when you had gone
Hang there still
Dropping one by one
As the year comes round again.

LONDON 31.7.79

Don't go combing your hair
When the sap is rising.
Chances are we'll
Never leave the bedroom
And your beautiful hair
Never leave the pillow.

INFINITE LOVER

So now I know.
And through all the things
That I have touched,
All that I have loved
(Or thought I loved)
Have brought me back... to you.

I can think of all the things
That I have taken into myself
And given out again,
Thinking that I know,
By some mis-used wisdom,
That I knew what love was.
I didn't —
And, perhaps, do not.

For although it has taken me
A lifetime to see in you
A universe of self-knowledge,
A wonder of love and truth
That extends beyond
What we seem to have shared,
I know now what blindness
Really is; what darkness
Really is; what stumbling
Really is.

So there you have it:
I am learning again
How to feel;
Learning how to know and accept
What is real;
And if Eternity and Truth
Are what I know them to be
Then do I know
That you still love me.

AND WHEN IT IS DONE

And when it is done,
The passion gone,
The smiles fewer,
Holding hands a rare event —
Where will we be then?

Looking into other eyes, other faces.
Watching other lovers;
Feeling again the ache of loneliness.

Does this mean that
We were lonely all along,
That what we had
Was just a ladder-rung
To some other lover?

I suppose it was...
But I would not have missed it,
Would you?

THE DOLL COLLECTOR

Every day those beautiful
Fifteen-year-old convent girls
Go sailing past.

I want to collect them like antique dolls
And decorate the house —
One for every room.

Antique dolls break easily
And fifteen-year-old convent girls
Tend to scream.

PARALLEL LINES

When I was a kid
There was something
Almost magical
About a train journey.
Those that I take now are few.

This one was magical too,
Yet different.

The line ran straight and true,
Through new-brick towns
And carefully considered gardens,
Parks set out like a regiment.
No smoke now, no magic haze;
The British Rail smell was
Now almost antiseptic;
The clickity-clack still there,
But different.

Then I saw it!
There in the undergrowth,
Another railway-line:
Overgrown, forgotten, weaving its
Way to dying, diminishing villages,
Forever fleeing to a smoke-filled past
Where the name Beeching
Never raised a curse.

My mind leapt from the train,
Leapt away, away, down that
Forbidden track. I needed no ticket now.

Men on coloured barges waved
Their hands; postmen on bikes
Rang handled bells; village
Policemen nodded; kitchen ladies,
Their hands weaving apple-pie,
Found time to throw a smile.

A hand on my shoulder:
"Ticket please!"

I looked out of the window.
The line had disappeared,
Running off, perhaps, into
Another dimension...
One that I could not follow...
   Or could I?

CLIFF'S REVENGE

The cliffs
Like chunks
Of broken cheddar
Gradually nibbled away
By the constant mouth of sea.

Remember me, cliffs?
Where is the shoe that I lost?
What use did you make of it?

What did you feel
As my lady and I
Worked our magical passion
In erotic frenzy
On your slopes,
And did the illegal smoke
Bring you joy?

What rage did you feel
When all your wildness
Was stripped, when uniform grass
Was laid to show off your curves?
I wonder, did the Council
Replant two trees
For every one
That they ripped from you?

Is that why
You are crushing
The concrete barriers
Set up to hold you in check?

SOMETHING THAT I NEVER KNEW
(For my niece Alexandra)

I found out today
Something that I
Never knew
In all my years:

I have in my possession
A giant who lives in the
Glove compartment of my car.

Also, I have been told,
There dwells a dragon in
A tiny bush in our back garden.

My pockets are full of fairy folk
And mice scamper in and out
Of my ears, hiding in my beard.

In my bed there lives a tiger,
In the wardrobe a lion
And in the woods a fairy princess.

Why have I been blind so long?
Why have I not known all these years?
It took a little girl of four
To take me by the hand... and show me.

First broadcast by BBC Radio Medway.

WHAT PRICE PERFECTION?

Such a day as this
I have never seen:

The sun shone like a
Bowl of cornflakes.
The wind fresh as
An aerosol spray.
The gentle rain
Like a cascade of Smarties.
The grass like Percy Thrower and ICI.
The clouds like instant mashed potatoes.

How perfect it all was.

Come the evening
The moon rose, huge and magnificent
Like a commercial for Ovaltine.

What perfection is this!
Who needs reality?

APPLE PIE MADNESS

Such an apple pie as never was:
  Baked to perfection,
Apples piled high with sugar 'cos
  Of soft browned fruit infection.

When seated in their place of office,
  Robed in pastry so fine,
Placed in the oven, not the hottest,
  I awaited this creation of mine.

Carefully timed, not a second more,
I gently opened the oven door:
Such a masterpiece I never saw;
Here was a baker who knew the score...
Till I dropped the bastard all over the floor!

First published by Gargantua *Magazine.*

THE HIGHWAYMAN

The Highwayman came riding
Over the misty moor,
He'd had his oats
In John O'Groats
And was riding back for more!

Broadcast 2 January 1978 on the BBC's Women's Hour *b*
The Barrow Poets.